"Alex Duke he[l
Bible at lightning speed, slowing down just enough for the reader to catch his breath to gaze at the beauty God's goal for creation. It contains sentences that will stick in the mind and convict the heart. *Nomad* helps to unlock the Scriptures, leaving you wanting to dig deeper into the Bible's pages. If you have ever felt like a wanderer, confused at what God is doing in the world, then let Alex Duke serve as your guide as he shows you the way home."

Dave Kiehn, Senior Pastor, Park Baptist Church; Director of Ministry: The Americas, The Pillar Network

"We're all born nomads seeking a way home, and the Bible points the way. With illustrations that will make you laugh out loud, Alex traces the path as he highlights God's faithfulness and goodness toward his people. *Nomad* is a great read that will give you the big picture and deepen your desire to open the Scriptures themselves."

Keri Folmar, Author of *The Good Portion: The Holy Spirit*; cohost, the *Priscilla Talk* podcast

"In *Nomad*, Alex Duke helps us see the Bible as one grand story: God's intention to dwell with his people in his place. Though human rebellion drove us into exile, Duke traces how God, through Christ, brings his people home again. If you're looking for a mercifully short and narratively refreshing way to help others grasp the story of Scripture, pick up this book and give it away."

Juan R. Sanchez, Senior Pastor, High Pointe Baptist Church, Austin, Texas; coauthor of *Reaching Your Child's Heart*

"In *Nomad*, Alex Duke sets out to consider the theme of God's people in God's place as a way of understanding the entire storyline of the Bible. Short but surprisingly comprehensive, reverent yet funny, insightful but easy to read, *Nomad* is a wonderful overview. Both new believers and longtime followers of Christ will benefit from thinking about the love of God that brings us into his presence forever. I highly recommend this book and will use it in my ministry."

Mike McKinley, Pastor, Sterling Park Baptist Church, Sterling, VA; author of *Friendship with God*

"Alex Duke is a skilled pastor, and in this book, he assists believers in understanding our place in the unfolding purposes of God. His approach is pastoral, as I would expect, and he seeks not only to educate believers but to assist them in becoming more faithful."

R. Albert Mohler Jr., President, The Southern Baptist Theological Seminary

"As followers of Jesus, we've all had moments where we felt out of place in this world. This book can help you understand what it means to feel displaced and alone and yet still find hope and purpose in this life for the glory of God. Be sure to get this book for yourself and more copies to hand out to others—it's relevant for everyone."

Shane Pruitt, National Next Gen Director, North American Mission Board (NAMB); author of *Calling Out the Called*

"The first question asked in the Bible is the question we all need to ask ourselves: Where are you? God knows where you are, but do *you* know where you are? Whether you feel hopelessly lost or content with the status quo, *Nomad* will help you find your place in God's story."

Gloria Furman, Author of *The Pastor's Wife* and *Missional Motherhood*

"*Nomad* is a wonderful, concise, and clear exploration of the biblical theme of exile—and the glorious return home through the saving work of Jesus Christ. Alex Duke has succeeded in helping his readers trace this theme through Scripture, and this little book will help many followers of Christ as they connect the redemptive dots throughout the arc of the biblical narrative. I commend this book to you."

Jon Nielson, Senior Pastor, Christ Presbyterian Church Wheaton (PCA)

NOMAD

A Short Story of Our Long Journey Home

Alex Duke

New
Growth
Press

newgrowthpress.com

New Growth Press, Greensboro, NC 27401
newgrowthpress.com

Cover Design: Derek Thornton
Interior Typesetting/Ebook: Lisa Parnell
Series Editor: Samuel L. Bierig

ISBN: 978-1-64507-521-9 (paperback)
ISBN: 978-1-64507-522-6 (ebook)

Library of Congress Cataloging-in-Publication Data on file

Printed in the United States of America

29 28 27 26 25   1 2 3 4 5

To Steve Hussung,
the aggressively ordinary pastor,
whose preaching opened up my eyes
to the beauty of God's Word.

The Road goes ever on and on,
Down from the door where it began.
Now far ahead the Road has gone,
And I must follow, if I can,
Pursuing it with eager feet,
Until it joins some larger way
Where many paths and errands meet.
And whither then? I cannot say.
— Bilbo Baggins

Contents

Introduction

A llow me to begin by stating the obvious: The Bible is not a short or simple book. It's both long and complex. It's comprised of many parts and was written over generations by the hands of a few dozen Spirit-inspired men.[1] The Bible is also not a uniform book. It's not a religious manual of rules or a spiritual guru's pithy insights or a divine and didactic lawgiver's code of conduct. Instead, it's more like the Cheesecake Factory menu, stuffed to the brim with wildly different genres of spiritual food: historical narrative, poetic prophecy, long speeches, genealogical data, military censuses, apocalyptic visions—and that's just in the Old Testament!

The Bible demands our attention primarily because it's inspired by the God of the universe. It's what the Creator of our consciousness wants us to be conscious of. The real God who really exists has really spoken, and we ought to listen. Because it's through listening to God's Word, that we learn about both who we are and who God is. By listening to God's Word, the static of this world begins to fade away and the most important stuff begins to stick out. What's more, God's Word repays whatever attention we give it a hundredfold. Its depth and beauty are inexhaustible because its Author's depth and beauty are inexhaustible.

We should give ourselves to the study of this book. Every phrase on every page tells us something about God, and therefore tells us something worth knowing, believing, trusting, and loving. "Great are the works of the LORD, studied by all who delight in them" (Psalm 111:2).

Now allow me to continue by stating something perhaps less obvious: The Bible is not an unknowable book. Its many parts add up to a unified whole. Its many genres take different routes to the same destination—some more scenic, others more straightforward.

The goal of this book is to chart one of the Bible's primary stories from beginning to end: the story of God's people in God's place. That's my straightforward, direct, no-frills answer. This book is about how God's people finally get to God's place.

This book will take a thoughtful route because our story is full of many, many, *many* ups and downs. It ebbs and flows and flows and ebbs and ebbs and flows again. The Old Testament, in particular, makes us feel its disastrous and dizzying recoil—as

God's people get to God's place and almost immediately get kicked out before they get back and eventually get kicked out again.

At times, the Bible's divinely inspired story arc might produce some feelings of hopelessness and angst as we accompany the nomadic journey of God's people. But then, at just the perfect time (Galatians 4:4), Jesus shows up to fix everything, to set God's people on the proper path toward finally returning to God's place once and for all. But his plan is unexpected; its ultimate fulfillment is delayed. It is, after all, a long journey home.

As you read, you might notice that Jesus doesn't appear in every chapter. This is intentional. The goal of this book is not to end every chapter with an alley-oop to Jesus. Don't get me wrong: All Scripture is about him, and all God's promises are ultimately *yes* in him (Luke 24:27; John 5:39; 2 Corinthians 1:20). These are beautiful truths.

But my main goal is to track the story of how God's people could return to God's place turn by turn. The story of the Old Testament is one of pent-up expectation for the coming Savior. Before his arrival, God's people went on a long, difficult, and often disastrous journey. The effects of sin's curse are pervasive in the Old Testament—and in our world today.

So when Jesus finally arrives on the scene, in God's sovereign timing, it elicits both incredible surprise and relief—for those who have eyes to see.

The birth, life, death, resurrection, ascension, and return of Jesus Christ, who is the God-Man, is the perfect answer to man's terrible problem: without Jesus, we would all be hopeless nomads forever.

Thankfully, that's not the story God has for us. Our story—for every true child of God—is one of incredible hope, joy, peace, and purpose, both now and in the life to come. Like ancient Israel, our earthly journey will be filled with many ebbs and flows. But our Guide is faithful and true. He will be with us every step until he brings us home to his place.

For now, we are still on the journey. As we travel, it helps to keep the big picture of God's grand story in view. So let's get started.

Chapter 1
Genesis 1–2:
Blessed in Paradise

The Bible begins with a trumpet blast: "In the beginning God created the heavens and the earth." By "the heavens and the earth," Moses means everything.

Throughout the rest of Genesis 1, we get a more detailed rundown. God created the sky and the stuff in the sky; he created the sea and the stuff in the sea; he created the soil and the stuff on the soil. He didn't need help, he didn't need time, he didn't need primordial ooze or a match to start a big bang.

God spoke, and it happened. Can you imagine the power? And all of it was "good" (Genesis 1:4, 10, 12, 18, 21, 25). It fit together perfectly. Can you imagine the wisdom?

God's creation project culminates with the creation of man. Here's how Moses records it:

> Then God said, "Let us make man in our image, after our likeness. And let them have dominion over the fish of the sea and over the birds of the heavens and over the livestock and over all the earth and over every creeping thing that creeps on the earth."
>
> So God created man in his own image,
>> in the image of God he created him;
>> male and female he created them.
>
> And God blessed them. And God said to them, "Be fruitful and multiply and fill the earth and subdue it, and have dominion over the fish of the sea and over the birds of the heavens and over every living thing that moves on the earth."
> (Genesis 1:26–28)

After stepping back to survey his handiwork, he looks at humanity and upgrades his evaluation from "good" to "very good" (1:31). And then he rests.

A SPECIAL STATUS AND A SPECIAL JOB

So that's it. That's the story of how God created humanity. We've been given a special status and a special job.[1] Our special status is that we've been created in the image of God. In fact, our special status enables us to do our special job: to rule ("have dominion"), to work and keep his creation, and to reflect God as we are fruitful and multiply, as we fill the earth and subdue it. Gnats and buffalo are free to fill the earth; badgers and stingrays are free to increase in number; Siamese cats and anacondas are free to multiply, though I wish they wouldn't.

But no animal is given dominion or stewardship because no animal is made in God's image. That responsibility of reflecting God to the world belongs to humanity and humanity alone. We are uniquely called to mirror God to the world as we rule over his world and cultivate his creation. We are the crown jewel of creation, the king of all the creatures.

At first glance, this opening chapter of Genesis seems almost stripped-down and utilitarian, like an entry-level textbook that tells the brief history of humanity. Here's how humans were made, and here's what humans are for. Where's the poetry? The art? The drama!?

For that we have to keep reading, because in Genesis 2 Moses zooms in on this creation story and gives us some colorful details.

First, he names the slice of earth in which he placed the nameless man: the garden of Eden (2:8). It's a lovely and luscious place, brimming with life. Then he names the man: Adam. He's there to "work" and "keep" the garden. And then, out of nowhere, the unbroken chorus of good-good-good screeches to a halt: "Then the Lord God said, 'It is *not good* that the man should be alone; I will make him a helper fit for him'" (2:18, emphasis mine).

To remedy this not-good situation, God creates Eve as Adam's helper. Together, they will fulfill humanity's responsibility. Together, they will be fruitful and multiply. Together, they will fill the earth and subdue it. Together, they will have dominion. What begins in the garden will extend to all creation. Or, more precisely, if humanity does their job, then the garden where God dwells with his people will grow and grow and grow and grow. By living in God's presence and under his providential care, it's as if paradise extends everywhere.

But God also gave Adam and Eve a commandment to follow:

> The LORD God took the man and put him in the garden of Eden to work it and keep it. And the LORD God commanded the man, saying, "You may surely eat of every tree of the garden, but of the tree of the knowledge of good and evil you shall not eat, for in the day that you eat of it you shall surely die." (Genesis 2:15–17)

As it turns out, humanity has a second job. In addition to working and keeping the garden of Eden, they must also listen to their Creator's word. They must trust him. They must believe that what he wants for their lives is better than anything they can do on their own.

EVERYTHING AS IT SHOULD HAVE BEEN

By the end of Genesis 2, God's people are in God's place. They are faithfully stewarding their role in the created order. The only people who exist are enjoying the Lord's presence without the static of sin or the consequences of rebellion. And it's moral perfection. It's marital bliss. They are, Moses tells us, "naked and not ashamed" (2:25).

God and his children regularly walked together in the cool of the day (Genesis 3:8). Can you imagine what they talked about? Can you imagine their mutual joy? Man and woman's unhindered fellowship with God and each other, delighting in his creation, enjoying the true satisfaction of accomplishing the good work God gave them to do? This is how it was meant to be. Can you feel the sense of belonging and peace described here?

Reading this may tug at your heart in a few ways. First, you instinctively know that this is what *you* were made for too: free, unashamed closeness with God. Doing what God gave you to do with joy. Knowing you are accepted and safe. Second, you know all too well that something's not right anymore. Your relationships suffer from brokenness. Your work may crumble. You feel like God is sometimes a million miles away. You struggle to feel at home. What now?

Right now, right in the middle of where you are, you can have hope: The God who spoke this world into being is committed to restoring all things. To making all things new. As we embark on the journey ahead, I'm going to lift the curtain just a bit: God's people are going to arrive back at God's place. It will happen. So, as you encounter people's brokenness throughout the arc of Scripture, as well as the brokenness you see inside yourself, you can take heart and watch for all the clues he gives us along the way—clues that point us to our true home and our true rest in him.

Questions for Reflection

1. What God wants for you and your life is always better than what you desire on your own. How do your daily choices agree or disagree with this truth?

2. Do you long for the unhindered fellowship with God that is described in Genesis 1–2? Or are you content with life as it is?

3. Where do you feel the brokenness of this world most acutely? What does Scripture have to say about that?

Chapter 2
Genesis 3:
Banished from Paradise

If Genesis 1 begins with a triumphant trumpet blast, then Genesis 3 begins with a more ominous overture. "Now the serpent was more crafty than any other beast of the field that the Lᴏʀᴅ God had made. He said to the woman, 'Did God actually say, "You shall not eat of any tree in the garden"'?" (Genesis 3:1).

Hang on, who is this fast-talking, lie-spitting snake?! Aren't Adam and Eve supposed to have dominion of the beasts of the field? Aren't they supposed to "work and keep" this garden by protecting it from harmful enemies like this?

We trust God's wisdom in revealing precisely what he reveals and withholding precisely what he withholds. There's so much we don't know about the "how" and the "why" of Genesis 3. But there's absolutely zero ambiguity about the "what." The seed of doubt that the serpent plants in Eve's mind blooms into a blasphemous weed that chokes out the bliss of human experience. In short, Adam and Eve sinned.

Sin. That's one of those words that different people use in wildly different ways. When Person A talks about "sin," they're talking about a bug in the system, a snag in the fabric, something regrettable and unavoidable in an otherwise worthy whole. When Person B talks about sin, they're talking about a terminal diagnosis, a bone-deep rebellion, a carried-on constitution that forever pits humanity against themselves and their Creator. Sin isn't merely a defect that makes us imperfect; it's a rebellion that dooms us—that breaks the fabric of who we are.

When the serpent urges Eve (and Adam) to sin, he's not merely urging them to break their divinely mandated diet. He's urging them to turn on their Lord, to try to take authority into their own hands and be gods. He's urging them to upend God's design for creation. Instead of having dominion over the animals, instead of working and keep the garden, Adam and Eve buy into the lie that they know better than God and that God doesn't have their best interests at heart. This is cosmic rebellion.

CURSES FOR REBELS

Once we understand what sin really is, the way God responds begins to make a bit more sense. He curses all the guilty parties. Let's look at what he says, first to the serpent:

> The Lord God said to the serpent,
>   "Because you have done this,
>   cursed are you above all livestock
>   and above all beasts of the field;
>   on your belly you shall go,
>   and dust you shall eat
>   all the days of your life.
>   I will put enmity between you and the
>   woman,
>   and between your offspring and
>   her offspring;
>   he shall bruise your head,
>   and you shall bruise his heel."
> (Genesis 3:14–15)

That last verse reverberates throughout the entire Bible. Basically, it says, "One day your head's gonna get crushed by a son of Eve." But for now, let's move on to God's curses to Adam and Eve:

> To the woman he said,
> "I will surely multiply your pain in
> childbearing;
>   in pain you shall bring forth children.
> Your desire shall be contrary to your
> husband,
>   but he shall rule over you."
> And to Adam he said,

"Because you have listened to the voice of
   your wife
      and have eaten of the tree
of which I commanded you,
      'You shall not eat of it,'
cursed is the ground because of you;
      in pain you shall eat of it all the days of
         your life;
thorns and thistles it shall bring forth for
   you;
      and you shall eat the plants of the field.
By the sweat of your face
   you shall eat bread,
till you return to the ground,
      for out of it you were taken;
for you are dust,
      and to dust you shall return."
      (Genesis 3:16–19)

The Crime, the Verdict, and the Sentencing

There's a lot we could say here, but for now let's observe three things: first the crime, then verdict, and then the sentencing. The crime is disobeying God's Word (Genesis 3:17).

The verdict, of course, is guilty.

But what about the sentencing? Hopefully you noticed that God's curses aren't random or haphazard. God's initial blessings now have an element of curse attached to them. Called to be fruitful and multiply, the woman is now sentenced to have her pain multiplied alongside her fruitfulness (3:16). Called to subdue the earth, the man is now sentenced to subdue an earth that fights back with thorns and thistles (3:18).

Is that it? No. Moses keeps going, and ends Genesis 3 with key information. The Lord's sentencing concludes, "Therefore the LORD God sent him out from the garden of Eden to work the ground from which he was taken. He drove out the man, and at the east of the garden of Eden he placed the cherubim and a flaming sword that turned every way to guard the way to the tree of life" (3:23–24).

Once blessed, now banished. That's the conflict at the center of this book—and it will take the rest of the Bible to fully and finally resolve it. We once dwelled in God's presence naked and without shame.[1] We were safe at home with the Creator of the universe, so long as we continued to trust him and listen to his word.

And then our rebellion wrecked the world. It ruined our relationship with the Lord. It cut us off and he drove us out—rightly so! More than that, he placed a sword-wielding sentinel to guard the entrance to his presence. We cannot get back through our own efforts, and if we try—we'll die. The wages of sin has always been death.

We were made to live alongside our Creator, to hear his footsteps as he walked beside us in the cool of the day, recognize his voice as he spoke to us. But Adam and Eve's rebellion has changed everything.

Their sin paved the way for our own. No matter how big or small they feel, our sins are the same crime as Adam and Eve's in the garden. They are rebellion.

As a result, whatever sinlessness Adam and Eve enjoyed has never been ours. They once lived at home *with God*. Not us. We were born "alienated" from God (Colossians 1:21).

In other words, since Genesis 3, we're all nomads—uprooted, trying to recapture the sense of home, seeking the fellowship and belonging we lost. Everything has changed.

QUESTIONS FOR REFLECTION

1. How do you see your sin in light of God's holiness?
2. At what points of your life have you felt most separated from God? How was close fellowship with him restored?

Chapter 3
Genesis 4–Exodus 13:
God's Work in Exile

Looking over the development of Scripture, we see that from Genesis 4 until the middle of Exodus, the theme of God's people in God's place recedes to the background. Why? Because before Moses gets to tell that story, he has to tell us how God's people Israel came to be a nation in the first place. In the story of Israel, we see the great lengths God went to in order to draw his people back to himself.

That's Genesis. It charts a path from Adam to Seth to Noah to Abraham to Isaac to Jacob to Jacob's twelve sons. Jacob also goes by the name Israel, so the account of Jacob and his twelve sons is also the story of Israel and its twelve tribes.

Throughout Genesis, the Lord makes all sorts of promises about these people who will come from Abraham's line. To Abraham he says,

- They will become a great nation (12:2).
- That nation will eventually become a conduit through which God will bless the whole world (12:3).
- Some of Abraham's offspring will be kings (17:6).
- This promise or covenant God is making is "everlasting." God promises Abraham that he will "be God to you and to your offspring after you" (17:7).

The Lord repeats versions of these same promises to Isaac and Jacob. We can summarize these promises as blessing, seed, and land. He will bless his people—as well as the outsiders who bless his people. He will plant seeds, establishing a lineage and an inheritance for his people. And eventually he will give them a land that is entirely their own.

God Didn't Leave Us on Our Own

Clearly, after exiling Adam and Eve out of Eden, the Lord didn't leave humanity to fend for themselves. He didn't consign us to a hopeless fate. He continued interacting with his creation, mercifully beckoning them to trust him.

As we read Genesis it's clear that if we want to be with the Lord, if we want to receive his blessing, then we should trust the promises he made to Abraham. We should trust his character: that he is good, he means what he says, he has compassion on our suffering, and he moves heaven and earth to draw us back to himself.

This might all sound really foreign and distant and abstract. Who's this guy telling me to "trust the promises he made to Abraham"? What does that even mean? I'm sympathetic to that instinct. But if that's what you're thinking, just remember that God's promises both to ancient believers and to us all prompt the same set of questions: Is the Lord trustworthy? Is following him worth it, despite the temptations to chart an easier path? What can I glean from the story of redemptive history that will give me hope in my struggles today?

As you continue to read, keep an eye out for something important: God's faithfulness. Neither the good nor the bad circumstances will stop God from working on behalf of his people, from mending the broken things, or from pointing his children toward home: a place where all wrongs are made right, exile is lifted, and God dwells in unbroken fellowship with humankind once again (and forever). No matter what his people do, God does not give up on them and does not let their sin have the final say.

GOD'S PLAN IN ACTION

By the time Genesis ends, the stage is set for the first phase of God's grand redemption that will come in Exodus. Of course, none of the principal characters have any idea that this is going to happen. They

can't tell the future, so they don't fully understand
the present. Joseph and his brothers have no idea
they're living through the golden era of Israel's relationship with Egypt. After all, Joseph is second in
command! The Israelites have their own area in
Egypt (Goshen) where they are free to live however
they please.

If you didn't know where the story went next,
then you might get to the end of Genesis 50 and
think to yourself, *Wait a second, have the promises the
Lord made to Abraham already come true!?* They've
got land on loan from Pharaoh, they're able to be
fruitful and multiply, and the promised blessing
seems to have been mediated from Abraham's
family to the whole world.

Aren't God's people finally in God's place?
Well, they're where they are supposed to be for a
season. But it's not their forever place. The land's
on loan from Egypt. They're renting a room. Joseph
knows this. He knows the fulfillment of God's
promises requires more than the peace they're cur-
rently experiencing.

All we need to do is look at his final words for
proof:

> And Joseph said to his brothers, "I am about
> to die, but God will visit you and bring you
> up out of this land to the land that he swore
> to Abraham, to Isaac, and to Jacob." Then
> Joseph made the sons of Israel swear, saying,

"God will surely visit you, and you shall carry up my bones from here." (Genesis 50:24–25)

LOOKING AHEAD TO A FUTURE HOME

Somewhere along the way, God spoiled the plot for Joseph. He told him about the upcoming exodus. That's why Joseph wants his brothers to swear to take his bones with him when they leave their temporary home and go to their promised home. But when will this happen? It's not immediately clear.

If you look at the opening verses of Exodus, it appears the descendants of Israel are picking up the mantle of Adam and Eve: They're being fruitful and multiplying. They've become exceedingly strong. They're filling the land. These Israelite image-bearers seem to be fulfilling their special job.

But then a new Pharaoh rises to power in Egypt—one who views the young Israelite nation as a threat. So he and the Egyptians "ruthlessly made the people of Israel work as slaves and made their lives bitter with hard service, in mortar and brick, and in all kinds of work in the field" (Exodus 1:13–14).

God gave Joseph the trajectory of Israel's redemption, but I wonder if he gave him the timeline?[1] From Exodus 1:1 to Exodus 1:14, Moses summarizes about four hundred years. The centuries have not been kind to Jacob's descendants; they've moved from welcome guests to unwelcome threats.

Their multiplication has enticed the Egyptians to murder; their fruitfulness has pushed Pharaoh to infanticide (Exodus 1:15–22). Where is God in all this? Has he left his people for dead?

No, he's preserving the life of their future liberator (2:1–22). He's not forgotten them even for a moment. I love how Moses pulls the camera's focus back and offers this delightful assessment during such a dark time:

> During those many days the king of Egypt died, and the people of Israel groaned because of their slavery and cried out for help. Their cry for rescue from slavery came up to God. And God heard their groaning, and God remembered his covenant with Abraham, with Isaac, and with Jacob. God saw the people of Israel—and God knew. (Exodus 2:23–25)

Did you notice how Moses reassures his audience that God's people still have his attention? No matter their circumstances, he hears them and he sees them. And now he's about to act on their behalf.

REDEEMING A PEOPLE FOR HIMSELF

Okay, *now* I'm pressing fast-forward. Let your mind's eye picture a sped-up Moses and Aaron as God uses them to unleash ten plagues on Egypt—from gnats to frogs to blood to boils to destructive hail to pitch-black darkness to Pharaoh's scream over the death of his and his countrymen's beloved sons. God orchestrated a display of his uncontested might and glory as he rescued his people from slavery.

Why did all this happen? The answer is multi-faceted: God was judging the hardness of Pharaoh's heart. God was keeping his promises. God was extolling himself as Yahweh, the one true God. But the reason most commonly shared in the text is that all of this happened for God's people, so that they might leave Egypt and serve the Lord. Notice how the Lord summarizes his motives:

- "Let my son go that he may serve me" (Exodus 4:23).
- "You shall say to [Pharaoh], 'The Lord, the God of the Hebrews, sent me to you, saying, "Let my people go, that they may serve me in the wilderness"'" (7:16).
- "Let my people go, that they may serve me" (8:1).

That third refrain gets repeated throughout the ten plagues (Exodus 8:20; 9:1, 13; 10:3). After Pharaoh's son died, after hemming and hawing and pump-faking obedience, Pharaoh finally gives in. He tells Moses and Aaron, "Up, go out from among my people, both you and the people of Israel; and go, serve the Lord, as you have said" (12:31). All of this happened so that the people of God could be plucked out of misery and replanted somewhere else. All of this happened so that they might serve the Lord.

After celebrating the Passover, the holiday in which Israel commemorated God "passing over" their homes during the final plague, Israel finally escapes the clutches of their centuries-long captors. And Moses makes sure to mention that he "took the bones of Joseph with him, for Joseph had made the sons of Israel solemnly swear, saying, "God will surely visit you, and you shall carry up my bones with you from here" (Exodus 13:19). As they were leaving Egypt, Israel remembered Joseph's long-ago last request.

Moses keeps going:

> And they moved on from Succoth and encamped at Etham, on the edge of the wilderness. And the LORD went before them by day in a pillar of cloud to lead them along the way, and by night in a pillar of fire to give them light, that they might travel by day and by night. The pillar of cloud by day and the pillar of fire by night did not depart from before the people. (Exodus 13:20–22)

Remember, the goal of this book is to track the movement of God's people back toward their home—back to being God's people in God's place.

In the beginning, the people of God were blessed to stand in the presence of God. Then we sinned and were banished from his presence. But God didn't give up on us. He didn't start over. Instead, he made a bunch of promises about how he would one day make a great nation from the offspring of a washed-up old man and his worn-out wife. The people who trusted these incredible promises experienced his presence—no, not precisely how Adam and Eve did in Eden, but they experienced his goodness nonetheless and were changed by it—drawn to want more.

By the end of Exodus 13, God's people are on the move again. Many decades would pass before they reached the land of promise that God had sworn to Abraham, Isaac, and Jacob. But God had graciously and mightily worked to redeem a people for himself, and he would faithfully keep every promise he made to an unfaithful people.

Aren't you glad that today God is still in the business of graciously and mightily redeeming a people for himself? Aren't you glad he still faithfully keeps every promise he has made to unfaithful people? Like ancient Israel, our sin and need for deliverance is great. But God's mercy, grace, and steadfast love are far greater. It was true thousands of years ago for the nomadic Israelites, and it's true for his people today.

QUESTIONS FOR REFLECTION

1. How have you seen God's faithfulness in your life even in the midst of your unfaithfulness toward him?

2. Why did God save Israel? What does your answer to that question reveal about your understanding of both God and salvation?

Chapter 4
Exodus 14–40:
A Traveling Worship Service

So far, we've been doing wind sprints. Running hard for a bit, then stopping; running hard for a bit, then stopping. In this chapter, we need to move into hyper speed as we follow the story of God's people in God's presence. I never really played sports so, to be honest, I know more about *Star Wars*' aerospace logistics than an athlete's training regimen.

Anyway, this chapter will travel to a few destinations and make a few clarifying digressions along the way.

Let me give you the bottom-line up front: The bulk of these chapters are devoted to the tabernacle instruction. The tabernacle becomes an extremely significant part of our story as the people of God. If God's first home with his people was the garden of Eden, his second home with them was the tabernacle.

We start at the base of Mount Sinai, in a remote mountainous region of modern-day Egypt. God's people are tired from the journey. They've just been rescued from under the thumb of Egypt. And yet, the people have grumbled to God and quarreled with Moses (Exodus 16). Oh, and Moses has complained about them too (Exodus 17:4). Put simply, things aren't going well.

At long last, they arrive at the base of Sinai. They set up camp as Moses goes up to God. Here's how he records the scene:

> The LORD called to him out of the mountain, saying, "Thus you shall say to the house of Jacob, and tell the people of Israel: 'You yourselves have seen what I did to the Egyptians, and how I bore you on eagles' wings and brought you to myself. Now therefore, if you will indeed obey my voice and keep my covenant, you shall be my treasured possession among all peoples, for all the earth is mine; and you shall be to me a kingdom of priests and a holy nation.'" (Exodus 19:3–6)

For the rest of Exodus, or at least most of it, God is speaking. And his opening statement—his preliminary remarks—is an overture on obedi-

ence. You will be my people *if* you obey my voice.
If you keep my covenant, you'll be my treasured
possession.

One problem with going through so much
Scripture so fast is that we will inevitably miss
some things along the way. So we might read this
section—and, really, several huge chunks of the
Law[1]—as one confusing, long list of how to get on
God's good side. But God's not a legalist. He's not
saying that the way into his favor is through our
behavior. No, the way into his favor was the same
then as it is now—it's through faith. Of course, true
faith reveals itself in obedience to God's Word. No,
not perfect obedience. But sincere, heartfelt, pro-
gressing obedience.

For now, it's worth noting that God's people are
standing at the base of a mountain. They're within
earshot of God's thundering voice; they tremble
(19:16–17). They cannot see a thing. Moses paints
the scene, "Mount Sinai was wrapped in smoke
because the LORD had descended on it in fire. The
smoke of it went up like the smoke of a kiln, and
the whole mountain trembled greatly" (Exodus
19:18). It's breathtaking. It's dangerous. So much so
that Moses has to tell the people to stay away lest
they die. Remember the angelic cherubim guarding
the holy garden? It's the same principle here. God's
mountain has become holy, so unholy people cannot
climb it.

A ROYAL PALACE AND ITS GUARDS

In Exodus 20–31, Moses records *a lot* of command-
ments. The first ten are well-known. For our purposes, we can skip them. We can also skip the laws on
altars and servants and donkey thievery and sojourners and sabbaths and festivals (Exodus 20–23).

Then in Exodus 24, Moses meets with God on
Mount Sinai, which is ringed in clouds, fire, and
smoke as God himself descends to dwell on this
mountain. For forty days, he and Moses meet face-
to-face. Why such a long meeting? Because what
God needs to tell him is both important and, to our
ears, a bit unusual.

I wonder if you tend to skim sections of
Scripture like Exodus 25–40. It's like an ancient
IKEA manual. Why do we need to know any of
this? We understand that it was important for
them then, but it doesn't seem important for *us now*.
But if we slow down and pay attention to a few of
the details, we might see things we've never seen
before.

First, let's look more closely at the ark of the
covenant. In Exodus 25:10–22, God gives Moses a
painstakingly detailed blueprint for the construction of the ark. The dimensions, wood type, gold
overlay, "mercy seat" instructions, special angelic
features for the lid, transport method—it's all there.

If the tabernacle is God's castle, the center of
the tabernacle is his throne room, and the ark of the
covenant is his throne—the seat of his power. You

might be welcomed into the king's house, but you wouldn't take that invitation as an excuse to sit on his throne. In other words, the ark is private, protected, and closed-off. You can't just check it out and open it up without getting your face melted off.

As you read this passage in Exodus, notice how Moses records the detailed design. It's wood covered with gold. But the top of the ark is pure gold and on top of the ark are two handcrafted cherubim of pure gold. The wings of these cherubim "overshadow" the ark, protecting and defending it.

Second, in Exodus 25:31–40, God gives Moses similar instructions for "a lampstand of pure gold," including details for "its base, its stem, its cups, its calyxes, and its flowers" (25:31). God says this special lampstand should have "six branches going out of its sides, three branches of the lampstand out of one side of it and three branches of the lampstand out of the other side of it," with "three cups made like almond blossoms, each with calyx and flower, on one branch" protruding from each side of the lampstand's center (25:32–33).

I hope you're still letting your mind paint a picture. It's as if Moses, the ancient IKEA manual writer, also has an MFA in poetry. His description of this lamp is chock-full of metaphors. This lamp has "flowers" and "branches" and "almond blossoms." Based on Moses's description, what is this lamp beginning to look like?

A tree.

Third, let's look ahead and see how Moses describes the work of the priests, whose job it is to make sure the tabernacle functions according to God's intentions. Exodus tells us what these priests should wear (Exodus 28) and how they are set apart for their important work (Exodus 29). Leviticus spends lots of time describing the kinds of offerings they bring on behalf of the people of God (Leviticus 1–15). In Numbers, however, we get a bit more narrative in which Moses describes the work of priests in an illuminating way.

According to the Lord, here's a priest's job description:

> And the Lord spoke to Moses, saying, "Bring the tribe of Levi near, and set them before Aaron the priest, that they may minister to him. They shall keep guard over him and over the whole congregation before the tent of meeting, as they minister at the tabernacle. They shall guard all the furnishings of the tent of meeting, and keep guard over the people of Israel as they minister at the tabernacle. And you shall give the Levites to Aaron and his sons; they are wholly given to him from among the people of Israel. And you shall appoint Aaron and his sons, and they shall guard their priesthood. But if any outsider comes near, he shall be put to death." (Numbers 3:5–10)

Do you see what this has to do with our task at hand?

In short, Moses describes the tabernacle as a new Eden. The ark of the covenant is guarded by cherubim, just like the entrance to the garden of Eden is guarded by cherubim. The Golden Lampstand is described as a tree, like the tree of life and the tree of the knowledge of good and evil. The priests are like Adam. Over and over, the Lord gives the Levites the same job as Adam in Genesis 2:15. They must *guard* and *keep* the tabernacle. Yes, in Genesis 2:15, the ESV describes it as "work" and "keep," but the underlying Hebrew verbs are the same.

A Glorious Place of Meeting

A few thousand years after Adam and Eve's sin, a few thousand years after God had cast sinful people out of his presence, he's now returned to dwell with them in the tabernacle.[2] An imperfect picture of God's perfect creation has reappeared. Just as Adam was to guard and keep God's temple in Eden, priests were to guard and keep the tabernacle.

Moses makes these connections on purpose. After recording God's detailed instructions in Exodus 25–31, he records a detailed account of Israel's obedience to those instructions in Exodus 35–40. Here's how the construction of the tabernacle concludes:

> According to all that the Lord had commanded Moses, so the people of Israel had

done all the work. And Moses saw all the work, and behold, they had done it; as the LORD had commanded, so had they done it. Then Moses blessed them. (Exodus 39:42–43)

Moses stands back to observe the tabernacle. This might remind us of the time the Lord stood back and observed his creation in Genesis 1. He saw the work and behold, it was good, because it was just as the Lord had commanded.

Then the tangible manifestation of God's glory comes back into view. God's glory "filled the tabernacle" (Exodus 40:34) so much so that Moses was not able to enter. "The cloud of the LORD" went before Israel in their journeys, and the "fire" of God's presence rested on the tabernacle at night (40:38).

Where does God live among his people? From creation in Genesis 1 to the fall in Genesis 3, the answer was "the garden of Eden." Now God lives wherever the tabernacle is, as long as God's people continue to offer their traveling worship, following the Lord's instructions by faith. As long as Israel actually meant it when they said, "What the LORD has said, . . . we will do" (Numbers 32:31).

Of course, God knows the end of Israel's story. He knows that they won't obey. He knows that their answer—"all that the LORD has spoken we will do" (Exodus 19:8; 24:3, 7)—is only sentiment. It's all sizzle and no steak. He knows they will sin and be scattered and exiled. He knows they will suffer in catastrophic, yet predictable ways (Deuteronomy 28:15–68). God even warns Israel about all of this centuries before any of it happens (Deuteronomy 4:25–30).

God *also* knows the *ultimate* end of the story. He knows that he will send his beloved Son to earth to obey in all the ways God's people didn't, suffer and die in all the ways God people deserve, and finally rise again so that God's people will know—once and for all—that sin's reign has ended. On that day, God's power over death has been demonstrated to the whole world.

QUESTIONS FOR REFLECTION

1. What did you learn about the tabernacle in this chapter? How does this institution illuminate for us what Jesus ultimately does for his people?

2. If it's true that God desires to dwell among his people, but sinful people cannot enter his presence, is there any hope for us? If so, what is it?

Chapter 5
Leviticus 1–1 Kings 4: A Traveling Circus

A s the Israelites travel toward the promised land, they vow, "What the LORD has said, we will do." As it turns out, they didn't really mean it. What the Lord said, they did . . . for a little while. Of course, there were some clues before God filled the tabernacle with his presence that the Israelites were a fickle bunch. The golden calf incident in Exodus 32 stands out. While Moses stood on the Mountain of God communing with God, they were busy blaspheming.

Later, when they are on the cusp of the Promised Land, the people hear an ominous report about what awaits them when they get there. So they grumble. They moan. They reminisce about Egypt with a serious case of revisionist history. And they even talk about replacing Moses with a leader who will guide them back into slavery.

Two guys who put together the Promised Land report—faithful Israelites named Joshua and Caleb—stand up and rebuke their countrymen for their lack of faith. They mean for their speech to be inspiring. It's not. Here's how Moses records their reaction: "Then all the congregation said to stone them with stones. But the glory of the LORD appeared at the tent of meeting to all the people of Israel" (Numbers 14:10).

When the Lord shows up this time, he's about *this close* from cutting them off and starting over. Ultimately, he renders a different judgment. He sentences them to wander in the wilderness for forty years until the disbelieving generation dies. Those who rejected God won't ever step foot inside the Promised Land.

This sentencing might seem harsh, but it's merciful. A punishment in the form of a "pardon" (Numbers 14:20).

What happens to the Israelites also happens to Korah's rebels (Numbers 16). I realize that "Korah's rebels" sounds like something out of a *Star Wars* movie. Well, the intergalactic resemblance continued when the splinter group who tried to usurp Moses's authority was ultimately swallowed up in the closest thing the Old Testament has to a Sarlacc pit.[1] Some survivors accuse Moses and Aaron—and, by implication, the Lord—of unrighteously stopping a *coup*. But it's clear that Israel doesn't fully understand the weight of this kind of rebellion. This episode warns against the presumption of believing yourself to be both wiser and more merciful than God.

Nothing has changed since the garden of Eden. Those who reject God's Word cannot sit idly by in his presence. Their faithlessness disqualifies them as God casts them out. The take-home lesson also hasn't changed: We must listen to God's Word. If we persist in rebellion and disobedience, he will make good on his promise to cut off those who reject him (Numbers 14:10; 16:19, 42). Sometimes, God makes good on this promise immediately (as with Korah and his rebels). Other times, the Lord's promise seems more protracted (as is the case with Moses's generation who wandered in the wilderness for forty years). But the principle remains the same. Just because we don't *immediately* suffer the consequences of our sin, doesn't mean the consequences aren't coming.

The construction of the tabernacle offered a solution to this problem. Thankfully, the tabernacle came attached to an instruction manual that explains how sinful people can persist in the presence of a holy God. But the construction of the tabernacle *by itself* could never fix the problem of sin. It was a temporary, impermanent solution, like a Band-Aid on an open wound.

Unfortunately, as we move further in Israel's history, they forget about God's instructions for the tabernacle. How do they treat this traveling temple of God once they finally do enter the

Promised Land? What should be traveling worship becomes, over time, a traveling circus. All rules go out the window for a time.

Let's try to follow the path this circus took. As we do, we'll see how God's people treated the tabernacle. What was supposed to be the sign of God's presence with his people became a distraction, an afterthought, and sometimes even worse.

Stop #1: In the Promised Land

Once Israel gets to the Promised Land, things start off quite well. In Joshua 3, the Israelites are no longer sojourners in a foreign land. They're no longer servants who, in addition to hard labor, receive room and board from their hard-hearted masters. They're *home*.

Did you notice what leads the way in this promise-fulfilling procession? What's the tip of the spear as God's people enter their enemy-occupied home? It's the ark of the covenant (Joshua 3:14). It's the Lord himself whose presence is carried along by his priests. His people follow from a distance.

God's presence, as manifested by the ark of the covenant, is integral to Israel's immediate success. If you're using an ESV Bible, the word "ark" shows up seventeen times in Joshua 4–6. It's there when the people fully and finally cross over the Jordan. It's there when they enjoy their miraculous victory over Jericho.

Even after Achan's sin in Joshua 7, Joshua and the other elders of Israel fall before the ark of the Lord (Joshua 7:6). Whether before victory or after sin, clearly the Israelites are treating their relationship with the Lord seriously, so much so that they renew their covenant. They build an altar and offer burnt offerings, and Joseph writes a copy of Moses's law on new stones (Joshua 8:30–32). Joshua concludes this beautiful, sobering scene with this detail:

> And afterward he read all the words of the law, the blessing and the curse, according to all that is written in the Book of the Law. There was not a word of all that Moses commanded that Joshua did not read before all the assembly of Israel, and the women, and the little ones, and the sojourners who lived among them. (Joshua 8:34–35)

Again, how beautiful. How sobering. This is the last time the ark shows up in the book of Joshua. In fact, we don't read about the ark again until Judges 20, a few hundred years later, when Israel is mourning in the midst of a civil war.

The authors of Joshua and Judges never explain what happened to the ark in all the intervening years (or centuries, more specifically). Instead, they allow the ark to recede into the background.

How do we explain this? Thankfully, the book of Judges gives us a clue in this repeated refrain, which doubles as an indictment against Israel: "In those days there was no king in Israel." This gets repeated four times (17:6; 18:1; 19:1; 21:25). Twice the author includes this sour addition: "Everyone did what was right in his own eyes" (17:6; 21:25).

So not long after Israel enters the Promised Land, they descend into a period where they have no Moses or Joshua-like figure to lead them. As a result, chaos reigns. Because Israel didn't have a king, they didn't have someone to do one of the king's main jobs: study and obey God's Word and transfer it to the people (Deuteronomy 17:18–20).

As we read through the dark book of Judges, if we're following the author's interpretive perspective, it shouldn't surprise us that obedience has receded into obscurity—and the ark with it.

The covenant ceremony in Joshua 8 signaled a renewed desire—albeit a temporary one—in God's people promising to take their relationship with God seriously. Their covenant is reminiscent of Exodus 20–24 or Deuteronomy 27–30. It's a return to form.

But from that point forward, basically until the end of the era of the Judges, Israel's relationship with their God deteriorated, and his dwelling in their midst became more and more diluted. In other words, they began to look just like the surrounding nations. Their light had been hidden under a bushel of their own disobedience and disinterest.

STOP #2: ON THE BATTLEFIELD

In 1 Samuel, which records the tail end of the judges era, the author paints a picture of both the good and bad in Israel. Let's start with the good:

Despite Israel's consistent rebellion against God as a nation, certain individuals remained faithful to him. For example Elkanah and his wife, Hannah, who committed their son, Samuel, into God's service. Samuel later became the final judge of Israel and anointed the nation's first king, Saul.

But trouble was never far away during this time. The high priest, Eli, lacked discernment, and his priestly sons abused their positions in greed, lust, and rejection of God's tabernacle instructions. We can read about this in 1 Samuel 1–2.

This picture is messed up because Israel is mixed-up. They have the outward appearance of conformity to God's law—there are priests, and the tent of meeting, and the ark; there are sacrifices, and people praying, and being dedicated to the Lord's service. Indeed, all the constitutive elements of obedience are there; the ark and all the appropriate apparatus are there. But it's hollow, empty, dead inside.

With the exception of one desperate, faithful woman (Hannah) who begs for the Lord's mercy, and for one miraculous son (Samuel) who loves the Lord so much that he sleeps at his feet, everything in Israel is rotten to the core.

So the Lord promises to reject Eli's house entirely. By now, Samuel is grown up and becomes "established as a prophet of the Lord" (1 Samuel 3:20). Israel is about to face the Philistines in battle. At first, it doesn't go well. Israel gets routed and loses four hundred men. The leaders are flummoxed. Here's how 1 Samuel 4 describes their response:

> Why has the Lord defeated us today before the Philistines? Let us bring the ark of the covenant of the Lord here from Shiloh, that it may come among us and save us from the power of our enemies." So the people sent to Shiloh and brought from there the ark of the covenant of the Lord of hosts, who is enthroned on the cherubim. (1 Samuel 4:3–4)

Do you see what's wrong with this picture? The author of 1 Samuel has already established for us that Israel is hollow and unholy. Only Samuel stands above the fray. And yet, in the face of bloody defeat, they think to themselves, "Wait a second! Why don't we trot the ark out here to help us win?" Clearly, Israel is treating the ark of the covenant like a lucky rabbit's foot. The author stacks the ark's honorific descriptors in 1 Samuel 4:4 on purpose—"of the Lord of hosts, who is enthroned on the cherubim"—as if to say, you can't treat this God so flippantly.

What happens next is predictable. The Israelites parade the ark to the battlefield, thinking it will be a token of good luck. But the Philistines rally to defeat Israel, kill thirty thousand soldiers and Eli's wicked sons, and capture the ark.

The lesson here is *not* that the Lord failed them. It's that the Lord will not be trotted out as a talisman to superstitious people with skin-deep faith. Later that day, a straggling, wounded soldier survives and manages to give Eli the bad news: Israel lost, his sons are dead, and the ark has been captured. Then the author of 1 Samuel closes the story by saying: "As soon as he mentioned the ark of God, Eli fell over backward from his seat by the side of the gate, and his neck was broken and he died, for the man was old and heavy. He had judged Israel forty years" (1 Samuel 4:18).

The Lord has kept his promise. Eli and his sons are dead. Notice that the author frames the story as if the ark itself finally deals the fatal blow. Eli, a man who sat idly in God's presence for so long, a man who got fat on ill-gotten sacrifice, now dies at the mere mention of the ark. The Lord always keeps his promises.

STOP #3: BEHIND ENEMY LINES

Once it's in Philistine hands, the ark's journey becomes increasingly comical—in a tragic sort of way. First Samuel 5 is like a scene from a

Charlie Chaplin film, or *The Three Stooges*. As it sits silently in a false god's temple, the ark keeps knee-capping the master of the house. The Lord keeps disarming Dagon, the Philistine's god. Of course he does—he doesn't want the Philistines to believe their victory over his faithless people meant a victory over *him*. The whole ordeal is hilarious to us, but it scares the Philistines so much that they pass the ark from city to city for seven months until they finally send it back to Israel where it belongs (1 Samuel 6:10–16).

STOP #4: OUT OF SIGHT, OUT OF MIND

But the ark's busy journey doesn't stop there. The Israelites, scared after seventy of them die "because they looked upon the ark" (1 Samuel 6:19), ship the ark yet again to Kiriath-jearim. They essentially say, *The Philistines sent this thing back to us, but would you please take it off our hands so we don't keep dying?* (6:20–7:2).

This might seem like a small detour, but the ark stays there *two decades*. The author of 1 Samuel understands the sadness of Israel's new reality: "From the day that the ark was lodged at Kiriath-jearim, a long time passed, some twenty years, and all the house of Israel lamented after the LORD" (7:2).

Do you know who doesn't get mentioned even once from 1 Samuel 4:1–7:2? I'll give you a hint: The book is named after him. That's right! Samuel vanishes while Israel vaults itself from superstition to stupidity to suspicion to sad indifference. When Samuel finally reappears, he has something to say:

> "If you are returning to the Lᴏʀᴅ with all your heart, then put away the foreign gods and the Ashtaroth from among you and direct your heart to the Lᴏʀᴅ and serve him only, and he will deliver you out of the hand of the Philistines." (1 Samuel 7:3)

Yet again—à la Joshua 8 and Exodus 34—the people repent and return to the Lord. How long will it last?

Sᴛᴏᴘ #5: Oɴ ᴛʜᴇ Gʀᴏᴜɴᴅ

To summarize 1 and 2 Samuel: Israel's hand-selected king, an impressive man named Saul, is bad. Israel's second king—an overlooked, unimpressive man named David—is (while still a sinful human) much better.

By the time we get to 2 Samuel 6, Saul is dead and David is king. David routs the Philistines on his way to be established as king in Jerusalem. But before he gets there, he wants to retrieve the ark from Kiriath-jearim after its two-decade stay.

But there's a problem: The men he sends to retrieve it don't know God's law. They don't know that Exodus 25 gives very specific details for how the ark is to be carried: on poles. So, when they "carry the ark of God on a new cart" (2 Samuel 6:3), we should hear the author's audible groan. They're doing the right thing but in the wrong way. So we shouldn't be surprised at what happens: The ark begins to fall and the Lord strikes Uzzah down for trying to stabilize it with his hand (2 Samuel 6:6–7). None of this would have happened if they'd followed the Lord's instructions.

Uzzah's mistake is the second offense, not the first. The first offense is treating the Lord's command and therefore his presence—here's that word again—flippantly. Uzzah is just as much a victim of the country and king's ignorance of God's Word, as he is a victim of his own over-eager presumption.

Stop #6: Finally at Home

It takes a while for David to get it. At first, he actually gets angry with the Lord for what happened (2 Samuel 6:8). Like the Israelites from the previous generation, he relocates the ark out of fear. But this time, rather than causing chaos and curses, the Lord blesses Obed-edom, the Gentile who takes him in (6:11).

Once he hears about Obed's blessing, David calms down and retrieves the ark. At long last—after centuries of unease and distrust, after generations of unbelief and disinterest—the king and his people finally usher the ark of God into the city of David.

Immediately, David notices an unrighteous contrast, that his home is nicer than his God's:

Now when the king lived in his house and the LORD had given him rest from all his surrounding enemies, the king said to Nathan the prophet, "See now, I dwell in a house of cedar, but the ark of God dwells in a tent." And Nathan said to the king, "Go, do all that is in your heart, for the LORD is with you."

But that same night the word of the LORD came to Nathan, "Go and tell my servant David, 'Thus says the LORD: Would you build me a house to dwell in?'" (2 Samuel 7:1–5)

God was about to significantly upgrade his special dwelling place among his people. But not yet. It would be in a time, place, and manner of his own choosing.

GOD WANTS OUR HEARTS

Yet as the anticipation builds in the Davidic reign—the short-lived pinnacle of ancient Israel's history—there are dark undertones. God's people repeatedly disobey God's Word. Every moment of spiritual triumph seemed to be sandwiched between bouts of tragic rebellion and disregard. The people often conformed outwardly to the tabernacle regulations, but their hearts were far from their righteous King.

God doesn't want lifeless, outward conformity to rules. He wants joyful, inward renewal of our hearts. In his mercy and grace, he chose to dwell among a stiff-necked and rebellious nation—a people very much like ourselves. He knows we—as spiritually dead wanderers—cannot bring about the radical heart-level change we need on our own. We need inner transformation that leads to outward change. We need a Savior. We need God to permanently dwell with us—and within us.

Questions for Reflection

1. Are there places in your life where you have the outward appearance, but not the real substance, of worship toward God? What should you do about that?

2. In your prayers or elsewhere in life, do you ever tend to treat God like a lucky rabbit's foot or talisman, hoping that he will magically give you what you want?

Chapter 6
1 Kings 5–10:
An Upgraded Address

I'll never forget our first apartment.

We rented one-and-a-half floors of a chopped-up, three-story house. We had our first baby there. I remember late nights and early mornings. I remember wondering if our neighbors across the hall could hear her scream and cry when Mom was gone and, like the typical brand-new dad, I couldn't figure out how to soothe her. A woman in her midthirties who loved to smoke weed and light candles lived below us. She had a gray streak in her black hair and my wife, Mel, once told me our downstairs friend was a self-proclaimed witch. She collected eggshells, as twenty-first-century witches are wont to do, I guess.

We had hodgepodge, mismatched furniture and the nicest cutlery and most pristine pots and pans you'd ever seen. We proudly wore this apartment as a badge of our blossoming, brand-new love. It was, after all, our home.

I'll also never forget our first real home.

It was a Cape Cod—I think that's what our realtor told us—near our church. It had the strangest basement I've ever seen, accessorized perfectly with a built-in bar that had a built-in TV that faced up toward the ceiling. The kitchen was tiny, the sinks drained too slow, the guest bedrooms kept a temperamental temperature, and the garage was absurdly oversized, which means we of course filled it with junk. What better badge for a maturing love than a garage filled with junk that you're unsure how you accrued, and even more unsure how to get rid of?

When something broke, I had to fix it. Correction: When something broke, I had to *pay* for someone to fix it. I had to mow the lawn, mulch the yard, unstop the sink, power wash the deck. I hated all of these tasks. But we loved having—owning—a home, a slice of earth we could call our own, something that would be as permanent as God's plans permitted.

From Exodus through 1 Kings 4, the Lord had a mobile home, the tabernacle. But the Lord always had something more permanent in mind for himself and his people (Deuteronomy 12:10–11). After all, if Israel was going to plant roots in the land of promise, they need to be rooted deeper than a few tentpoles in the dried-out soil.

At the end of the last chapter, we saw how David felt uneasy about having a palace nicer than the Lord's house. He tells the prophet Nathan, "I dwell in a house of cedar, but the ark of God dwells in a tent" (2 Samuel 7:2). Surprisingly, the Lord tells David that he is disqualified from this construction project because he has blood on his hands (1 Chronicles 22:8). The task falls to his son Solomon instead.

The Bible tells this story twice: in 2 Chronicles 2–5 and 1 Kings 6–8. We'll focus on the latter. But what we need to notice is just how connected these passages are to Exodus 25–40 and Genesis 1–3. Just as the tabernacle was a new Eden, so the temple is a new Eden—in fact, we might say it's *the* Eden that the whole Old Testament had been anticipating.

We see the culmination of this story in 1 Kings 8:1–11. The scene is remarkable. As Solomon and all of Israel look on,

> the priests brought the ark of the covenant of the Lord to its place in the inner sanctuary of the house, in the Most Holy Place, underneath the wings of the cherubim. . . . And when the priests came out of the Holy Place, a cloud filled the house of the Lord, so that the priests could not stand to minister because of the cloud, for the glory of the Lord filled the house of the Lord. (1 Kings 8:6, 10–11)

The entire Old Testament has been leading up to this moment. The Lord moving in to his permanent home. He has finally upgraded his address.

The cherubim guard the Lord's throne at the heart of the Lord's home, just like the garden of Eden. A cloud came down from heaven to signal his unapproachable presence, just like on Mount Sinai.

For the rest of 1 Kings 8, King Solomon is a righteous king. He prays a beautiful prayer and offers abundant sacrifices. He blesses the Lord and his people.

Where will God's people dwell in peace with him? For now, in his temple, his home, where so many sacrifices are offered up to him in faith.

And guess what happens immediately after the temple's dedication? The queen of Sheba shows up, and seems to become a worshipper of the Lord (1 Kings 10:1–13). In the language of the prophets, we might say the nations are streaming to the mountain of the Lord (Isaiah 2:1–5). Or, in the language of Moses in Genesis, we might say the Lord has made Israel a great nation that is blessing all the families of the earth (Genesis 12:1–3).

This is exactly how it should be. Isn't this a picture of what we all want in our lives today? Peace. Security. Blessings. Hope. To feel—and perhaps even see!—the glory of God in our lives. To sense his presence. To feel at home with him, like we are exactly where we are meant to be.

Oh, if only the story stopped here.

QUESTIONS FOR REFLECTION

1. God's people are always blessed when he lives among them. What are some of the blessings you've received from God's presence in your life?

2. David realized that he lived in a house of cedar while God "lived" in a tent. Do you fully appreciate God's presence in your life, or are you simply going about your life trying to build your own little kingdom?

3. When was the last time you truly paused to reflect on God's continual presence with you and enjoy the sweetness of genuine worship?

Chapter 7

1 Kings 11–Malachi 4:
An Eviction Notice

King Solomon truly had it all.

The author of 1 Kings offers a striking description of Solomon's early days in 1 Kings 10:14–29. Solomon's annual gold imports were 666 talents—an unfathomable amount. His throne was made of pure ivory overlaid with gold. All his drinking vessels were gold. He had gold military shields on display—just because he could. In fact, gold was so plentiful during Solomon's reign that silver was virtually worthless. Solomon also owned a stockpile of chariots, horses, and even exotic animals. Merchants and dignitaries from around the ancient world flocked to meet with him, marvel at his wealth, and hear his wisdom.

At this point in history, Israel's GDP is booming. Their reputation on the global stage is pristine. This is Israel's golden age. Right?

In reality, the author's intention is precisely the opposite. In Deuteronomy 17:14–20, generations before the prohibition could be either obeyed or ignored, the Lord warned Israel *not* to rely on a king who relied on his stuff—his gold and silver, his horses and chariots. He warned these kings not to multiply wives, because the Lord knew that multiplied wives divides a king's allegiance to the Lord.

Of course, the author of 1 Kings doesn't begin his narration with an explicit reference to Deuteronomy 17. But he expects his readers to be aware of what that passage says. He expects his readers to get a lump in their throat as they read about Solomon's accumulation of neutral things in 1 Kings 10—horses, chariots, gold, etc. What's impressive also have been ominous.

By listing these material blessings, the author of 1 Kings primes the pump for what's to come. In other words, 1 Kings 11 isn't a contrast to Solomon's earthly success, but a result of it. This is where we read about Solomon's "700 wives, who were princesses, and 300 concubines" (11:3). There was a deep spiritual problem here, "for when Solomon was old his wives turned away his heart after other gods, and his heart was not wholly true to the LORD his God" (11:4). Tragically, Solomon worshipped the abominable false deities of the surrounding nations and even built altars for the detestable gods of Moab and Ammon.

A reign that had started off so well—with the building of God's temple—had devolved into terrible heathenism. "And the Lord was angry with Solomon, because his heart had turned away from the Lord, the God of Israel, who had appeared to him twice and had commanded him concerning this thing, that he should not go after other gods" (1 Kings 11:9–10).

What a downfall. How quickly, in the author's retelling, does it seem that the mighty have fallen. But more likely, the fall was slow—not sudden. Upon acquiring all these wives and concubines, King Solomon's heart drifted away. The wise king descended into wickedness. By the end of 1 Kings 11, Solomon is dead (11:41–43). Compared to the accounts of David, the author dispatches Solomon rather quickly.

A DESCENT INTO EXILE

Throughout the rest of 1–2 Kings, we see that though the temple was a remarkable achievement, it couldn't fix the problem of sin.

Rather quickly, Israel splits between the North (Israel) and South (Judah). In 1 Kings 12:25–33, King Jeroboam of Israel builds a rival temple in Shechem. Almost overnight, he leads the Israelites into pagan worship that is laughably close to the chaos of Exodus 32. During Jeroboam's reign, the original temple in Judah gets littered by cult prostitutes and looted by an Egyptian pharaoh (1 Kings 14:21–28).

Less than a century later, King Ahab of Israel and his wicked wife Jezebel build a rival temple for a rival god, Ba'al (1 Kings 16:32). Thankfully, it does eventually get torn down (2 Kings 11:18).

A few decades later, about 150 years after Solomon initially built the temple, King Joash of Judah repairs it (2 Kings 12:4–16). Unfortunately his reign doesn't end well, as he eventually allows Baal and Asherah worship in the land (2 Chronicles 24:17–19) and gets assassinated (2 Kings 12:20). His son Amaziah eventually gets captured by the king of Israel who ransacks the temple and returns to Samaria.[1]

After a visit to Assyria, King Ahaz of Judah decided to desecrate the temple and build his own altar instead (2 Kings 16:15–18; 2 Chronicles 28:24–25). His son King Hezekiah, under threat from Sennacherib of Assyria, stripped the temple for parts, taking the gold off the doors. He does so in order to appease a foreign king (2 Kings 18:13–15). Later on, after Sennacherib gets his cut, Hezekiah will be much more materially prosperous—so much so that he'll show off before some Babylonian envoys. The prophet Isaiah takes Hezekiah's bluster as an opportunity to tell him about his kingdom's eventual exile into Babylon, during which they will lose all the material things they gained (2 Kings 20:12–21).

1 Kings 11–Malachi 4: An Eviction Notice

Hezekiah's response is as jaw-dropping as it is sad: "Who cares? I'll be dead then anyway."[2]

Hezekiah's son King Manasseh is perhaps the worst of the bunch. He put pagan altars *inside the temple* (2 Kings 21:1–9), and even sacrificed his son on one of them. The author of Kings is so disgusted by this that throughout his retelling he reminds the people of Israel just how far they've fallen from the Lord's original designs (vv. 4, 7–8).

As 2 Kings comes to a close, we read about Manasseh's son King Josiah. Much to our surprise, he's a good king. He is committed to repairing the temple, returning it to its past glory. As he does, much to *his* surprise, they find the book of the law (2 Kings 22:3–11). When Hilkiah the high priest reads it to Josiah, the king tears his clothes and weeps. He laments that, quite obviously, "Our fathers have not obeyed the words of this book" (22:13).

Josiah is the closest thing 1–2 Kings gets to a paradigmatic, Deuteronomy 17 king. He rediscovers the word, reads it before the people, and urges them to keep it. He destroys every hint of his grandfather Manasseh's idolatry (2 Kings 23:1–20). He restores the Passover, which hadn't been practiced since the day of the judges (23:21–27). Finally, the author has a reason to heap praise instead of disgust: "Before him there was no king like him, who turned to the LORD with all his heart and with all his soul and with all his might, according to all the Law of Moses, nor did any like him arise after him" (23:25).

And yet . . . despite this spiritual renewal, God still keeps his word to Hezekiah. Jerusalem is captured.[3] The temple's vessels of gold are chopped to pieces and divvied up among the pagans (2 Kings 24:13). Along with the house of the king, the house of the Lord is burnt to the ground (25:9). The bronze that covered the temple's pillars gets carried off to Babylon (25:13). The dwelling place of God is fully and finally ransacked (25:13–17).

Why are we talking about the terrible ways that terrible kings treated God's temple? Because Israel's kings stood in the place of the nation as a whole. Generally speaking, the way they treated God reflected the people's sentiment toward God.

It's no surprise that this story ends in exile. History repeats itself. Just as the people of God were exiled from God's presence for their sin in Genesis 3, so the people of God are exiled from God's presence for their sin in 2 Kings 25. The Babylonians are but an instrument in the Lord's hand, the means by which he keeps his word to them in Deuteronomy 4:25–28. There's a reason Josiah trembled when he finally found the word of God. He knew what was coming. He knew they were cooked. He knew their sins were many and God's promises were sure. He knew they'd scorned the blessings of the covenant and were about to stand face-to-face with the curses of the covenant (Deuteronomy 27–28).

What the people had said they would do, they did not do. What their kings had promised to do, they had not done. So it was only a matter of time.

THE GLORY DEPARTS

The author of Kings isn't a news anchor or beat writer. He's a historian. He's got a job to do: This happened, and then this happened, and then this happened. He provides subtle contextual explanations along the way, giving the "why" almost as often as the "what" to his original readers, many of whom had grown up learning the Scriptures prior to 1–2 Kings.

Thankfully, the Bible is such an amazing book that it gives us another interpretive perspective of these same events. Again, 1–2 Kings and 1–2 Chronicles are historians' renditions of these events. The prophetic books belong to the poets and the artists. This is especially true of the big three: Isaiah, Jeremiah, and Ezekiel. They have the widest aperture and grandest scope. But it's true to some degree of all the prophets, even those that comment on narrower events.

One of these prophets is a man named Ezekiel. The Lord gives him a vision just before the Babylonians invade. Here's how he poetically narrates the sad conclusion of Israel's history:

> And the cherubim mounted up. These were the living creatures that I saw by the

Chebar canal. And when the cherubim went, the wheels went beside them. And when the cherubim lifted up their wings to mount up from the earth, the wheels did not turn from beside them. When they stood still, these stood still, and when they mounted up, these mounted up with them, for the spirit of the living creatures was in them.

Then the glory of the LORD went out from the threshold of the house, and stood over the cherubim. And the cherubim lifted up their wings and mounted up from the earth before my eyes as they went out, with the wheels beside them. And they stood at the entrance of the east gate of the house of the LORD, and the glory of the God of Israel was over them. (Ezekiel 10:15–19)

Don't let the disorienting details blur the main image: The cherubim, the guards of God's presence in the Holy of Holies, retreat from their post as his glory departs from the temple.

Again, it's like we're back to post–Genesis 3. There's no temple, no tabernacle. There's barely even a nation. The vast majority of Israelites are exiled in Babylon. There is no place for the people of God to dwell peacefully with him. In fact, there hardly seem to be any people of God at all.

A GLIMMER OF HOPE

It's probably not a stretch to say that everyone—Christians and non-Christians alike—have felt like God has abandoned them at some point in their lives. When have you felt this way? Was it after the death of a child or a loved one? During a bitter divorce? Amid severe health issues or financial challenges?

If you've ever felt this way, you're in good company. This was the cry and concern of many Old Testament prophets. The books of Job and Lamentations explore this issue significantly. The apostle Paul described a particularly difficult time in Asia as follows: "We were so utterly burdened beyond our strength that we despaired of life itself" (2 Corinthians 1:8).

Thankfully, God never abandons his children. Does he allow trials in our lives? Yes. Does he use hardship to refine our spiritual character? Absolutely. But his glory never departs from those who truly call on his name. As Deuteronomy 31:8 says, "It is the LORD who goes before you. He will be with you; he will not leave you or forsake you. Do not fear or be dismayed."

Unfaithful Israel learned a tragically hard lesson. But through Ezekiel and other faithful prophets, God delivered a message of future hope. Like most good poets, biblical prophets didn't just narrate the news. They reflected on the past and present with an eye toward the future. They had a hunch that what was happening in the present wouldn't always be. The Lord allowed them to crane their necks into the future to see a restored Israel, even amid the devastating destruction.

The last paragraph of the book of Ezekiel, in chapter 48, describes the future city of Israel's divine King, and his restored temple within it. After many visions and oracles of judgment and woe, the exiled prophet ends with this hope-filled note: "And the name of the city from that time on shall be, The Lord Is There" (v. 35).

God's restored temple doesn't sit on an island, or alone in a field. It sits at the center of a perfect city; its God-centered influence has extended far beyond its walls. And this city's name is a beautiful one, especially for those who've just witnessed the Lord's departure: "the Lord is there."

But when will he come?[4]

Questions for Reflection

1. Have you ever felt like God's glory has departed your life? How did the truth of God's Word steady you during that difficult time?
2. During the trials you've experienced in life, what have you learned about yourself? What have you learned about God?

3. The tabernacle didn't fix Israel's problem of sin. Neither did the more permanent temple, nor even the Old Testament law or the sacrificial system. If this God-given spiritual help didn't solve humanity's sin problem, what will?

Chapter 8
Matthew 1–John 21: An Exile in Reverse

I suspect it would take most people about ten seconds to flip from Ezekiel to the New Testament. How convenient. And yet, it's worth mentioning that Ezekiel penned those hope-filled words in Ezekiel 48:35 in 573 BC. So this promise to Israel hung in the air *for centuries*. It lingered through exile, through temple building, through prophets as far as Malachi, and then, finally, through the silence of God.

The Lord had departed from the temple, and the insufficiency of its replacement made the people weep (Ezra 3:12–13). The Lord's people were overrun by invaders and outsiders; generations pass, and even Israel's invaders are overrun by outsiders.

When we get to the New Testament, Israel is under the thumb of a different nation—Rome—which didn't even exist when the people of God first built the temple of God.[1] Ezekiel's stirring promises surely seemed like distant memories at best, or coping mechanisms at worst; old stories that their grandparents told themselves to maintain their identity as Israelites.

When will the Lord return? Where—in the midst of all this rubble, in the face of all these dusty promises—can God's people dwell at peace with him?

If you asked most Israelites at the turn of the millennium, I wonder how they would have responded. Some would have answered with a silent shrug. Some would have felt that the question itself posed excessive, unnecessary optimism. A select few would have lit up: *I don't know when and I don't know where, but I know that God always keeps his promises.*

Against this backdrop, this is how the apostle John describes Jesus at the beginning of his Gospel. He refers to Jesus as the Word who is from the beginning (John 1:1), and who was with God in the beginning (v. 2). Then John ups the ante: This Word *was* God from the beginning (v. 1). He had a preeminent, necessary role in the creation of "all things" (v. 3). He is "light" and "life" (v. 4).

And now, the one who has created the world has come into the world to be rejected by the world—worse, to be rejected by his own people (vv. 9–11). But some will receive him, believe in his name, and as a result, become children of God (v. 12).

Here's how John closes his prologue:

And the Word became flesh and dwelt among us, and we have seen his glory, glory as of the only Son from the Father, full of grace and truth. (John bore witness about him, and cried out, "This was he of whom I said, 'He who comes after me ranks before me, because he was before me.'") For from his fullness we have all received, grace upon grace. For the law was given through Moses; grace and truth came through Jesus Christ. No one has ever seen God; the only God, who is at the Father's side, he has made him known. (John 1:14–18)

Think about the testimony of Scripture so far. No one has ever seen God. Not Adam and Eve, not Abraham, not Moses or David or Solomon. But in Jesus, the unseeable has been revealed to the children of God.

John, in the grand opening of his Gospel, affirms that Jesus is the eternal Son of God—a full member of the immortal Trinity—and that in his incarnation, he became God in the flesh, perfectly revealing who God is: fully human and fully divine.

So, once we get to the New Testament, where does God dwell? Not in a place—Eden or the tabernacle or the temple. No, he dwells in a *person*. In fact, he *is* a person—Jesus Christ!

THE UNEXPECTED ARRIVES

No one expected this. We could never have fath-
omed that God would have orchestrated such a
perfect miracle. Of course, we knew what Solomon
knew way back in 1 Kings 8. We knew that the God
of the universe couldn't be contained by mere bricks
and mortar, even if they were divinely decreed.

John 2 makes this connection between Jesus
and the temple even more explicit. After Jesus turns
water into wine, he heads to Jerusalem with a single
mission on his mind: to visit the temple and, after
seeing that it had become a place of greed and com-
merce, judge the temple.

In John 2, the real temple invades the obsolete
one—and he doesn't like what he sees. I suppose
money laundering is better than Manasseh's child
sacrifice, but only by degree not by kind. The
temple has become a godless place for godless activ-
ity. So Jesus empties pockets and overturns tables
(v. 15). He quotes Scripture and makes a scene,
which his disciples recognized as a sign of his deity
(vv. 16–17).

When Jesus cleans house, it's like an exile in
reverse. God himself enters the temple and forces
all the God-impostors to leave. He's moving back in.
They don't like this at all, so they ask him to basically show his credentials. *Who do you think you are?*
they hiss (v. 18).

Jesus responds with an enigmatic, but powerful statement: "Destroy this temple, and in three days I will raise it up" (2:19). They're confused. What kind of architectural trick does this guy have up his sleeve? They respond, confused, "It has taken forty-six years to build this temple, and will you raise it up in three days?" (v. 20).

John doesn't record the end of this tense conversation. He doesn't tell us how Jesus responds. Instead, he pulls the camera back to make the implicit explicit, to make the subtle sublime. He writes, "But [Jesus] was speaking about the temple of his body. When therefore he was raised from the dead, his disciples remembered that he had said this, and they believed the Scripture and the word that Jesus had spoken" (vv. 21–22).

What a remarkable revelation. Jesus tells Israel's scriptural guides—those most acquainted with how God has dealt with his people throughout history—precisely what's going to happen next. In other words, what Jesus's body will endure as a result of Israel's sin is a microcosm of Israel's own history. He will be torn down only to be raised up again. But when people see his raised body they will not cry out in frustration because the new is not like the old (Ezra 3:12). Instead they will cry out in faith because the new is not like the old. Jesus is a better temple for a better covenant.

A Better Temple in a Perfect Person

Why is Jesus a better temple? There are at least two reasons. First, because there's no longer any distance between the sign and the God it signifies. Eden wasn't God; the tabernacle wasn't God; even the temple at its height wasn't God. These were unique places in which God manifested his presence to his people. God *dwelled* there, and mercifully so. But Jesus? He *is* God. The *fullness* of God is pleased to dwell *in him* (Colossians 1:19–20).

Second, because we are no longer required to offer any sacrifices of our own. Consider the climax of Jesus's conversation with the Samaritan woman at the well in John 4. She's concerned about the logistics of worship—should she worship at the ancient Samaritan mountain of worship on Gerizim, or the Jewish temple mount in Jerusalem? But Jesus is concerned about the *focus* of worship. No matter *where* worship happens it must come from the heart; it must be in spirit *and* truth; and it must be centered on God himself. It must trust his word as the Messiah (John 4:26).

With Jesus's arrival, there is a sudden paradigm shift when it comes to worship: We don't need to bring the right sacrifice to the right priest at the right time in order to enjoy right standing before God. Instead, we simply must trust that Jesus's sacrifice is fully and finally sufficient. We must rely on him. We must resist any urge to save ourselves through our morality or our hard work or our right theology. We must fully and finally depend on Jesus as our only hope.

Consider Paul's charge to the Christians in Rome: "I appeal to you therefore, brothers, by the mercies of God, to present your bodies as a living sacrifice, holy and acceptable to God, which is your spiritual worship" (Romans 12:1). Wait a second. A living sacrifice? This might sound like an oxymoron, but it makes complete sense when we understand the person and work of Jesus.

When Jesus died, the curtain of the temple was torn in two and access to God was wide open (Matthew 27:51; Mark 15:37–38; Luke 23:45–46). The mercies of God provoke us to present not a bird or a bull, but our very bodies to him as proof that we trust him. And we must get this order right: God's mercy first, our response of worship second. Our worship doesn't provoke God to be merciful to us. God's mercy to us provokes our worship.

In the New Testament, where do God's people dwell in peace with him? As the story of Scripture advances, the answer becomes a bit inexact. It's no longer a *where*, but a *who*. God's people dwell in peace through faith in Jesus. He is the only operational temple now. The other one is obsolete.

For three years during his earthly ministry, Jesus perfectly revealed who God is and what God is like, since he is God himself—the second Person of the Trinity, God in the flesh. But hang on. Jesus is no longer here on earth. He's not standing at attention somewhere in the outskirts of Jerusalem, beckoning travelers and nomads to walk by and see what God is like. No, he's ascended into heaven. He's sitting at the right hand of his Father (Hebrews 10:12–14; Revelation 3:21).

So where do the travelers and nomads look *today* if they want to know what God is like?

Questions for Reflection

1. How did Jesus's life, death, and resurrection shift the paradigm of human worship forever? How should it affect *your* worship?

2. How does the truth that God's mercy to us provokes our worship (rather than vice versa) cause you to think about your own worship?

3. The question that many first-century Israelites were asking—"When will the Messiah come?"— is on the lips of every Christian today as we await Jesus's second coming. What Scripture passages can help you wait with joy, hope, and obedience?

Chapter 9
Acts 1–Jude 1:
The Familiar

We have two more stops on our journey home. The first will be familiar to you; the second and final stop will seem so fantastic that it will seem almost fake, too good to be true. But we'll save that for the last chapter.

First, the familiar one. Let's turn to 1 Corinthians 3, where Paul is making a plea to a divided church. This church is full of "jealousy and strife" (1 Corinthians 3:3). They're full of factions (v. 4). They're acting more like mere humans, giving in to the flesh and not paying attention to the Spirit's work (vv. 1–3).

To fix this division, Paul reminds them of what they are, now that they're all in Christ. He doesn't use an adjective—you're *new*, you're *holy*, you're *rebuilt*. Instead, he uses a metaphor: you are

God's building (v. 9), whose foundation is Jesus Christ. On the last day, the fire will reveal what's been built on this foundation with gold, silver, and precious stones, and what's been built with wood, hay, and straw (3:10–15). Put simply, we shouldn't fight over fruitfulness and effectiveness because it's God who decides what work endures and what doesn't.

Then Paul asks an enlightening question: "Do you not know that you are God's temple and that God's Spirit dwells in you? If anyone destroys God's temple, God will destroy him. For God's temple is holy, and you are that temple" (1 Corinthians 3:16–17).

A Temple and a Lighthouse

I grew up in Kentucky, when it was laughably common for teenagers to smoke. Maybe not habitually, but at least recreationally. It was the Bluegrass rite of passage. While it would be a lie to say I *never* partook, it would be true to say that I was never at risk of becoming "a smoker." Who can say why? Perhaps it was because I always heard, in the back of my head, a Sunday school teacher or small-group leader tell me I should never smoke cigarettes because "your body is God's temple." They were probably right, and my lungs appreciate the admonishment. But that's absolutely *not* what Paul is talking about in 1 Corinthians 3.

He means that the gathered people of God in Corinth, the "church of God that is in Corinth" (1:2), they *together* are God's temple. God dwells on earth *among them* as a church.

Throughout 1 Corinthians, we see how this reality of the church as God's dwelling place is supposed to shape their life together. Here are two similar examples:

- In 1 Corinthians 5, Paul rebukes the church for not doing what it should be doing, and for letting sin persist unchecked. Since they are God's temple, they must assemble in God's name and remove the man who's happily sleeping with his mother-in-law. Of course, churches are open to all manner of sinners, but they should only feel like home to those eager to turn from their sin and embrace Jesus as their Savior.

- In 1 Corinthians 6, the church *is doing* what it *shouldn't* be doing. Instead of confronting sin like Christians, they're taking each other to court and letting their disputes be judged by the world. They're also treating sexual sin too flippantly.

Put simply, because the church is the temple of God, the church's relationship to sin must radically change. It must be at war, not peace, with sin.

This image of the church as God's temple shows up elsewhere in the Bible to different ends. In Ephesians 2, Paul uses the metaphor to remind the church of their unbreakable unity.

The work of Jesus on the cross has killed whatever hostility persisted between Jew and Gentile and, in the same moment, created "one new man." This work is the cornerstone of the new-covenant temple of God, whose bricks are made up of both Jews and Gentiles—all who have been saved by grace through faith (Ephesians 2:1–10; 1 Peter 2:1–4). Ephesians 2:11–22 is full of temple language, including concepts such as the dividing wall of hostility, strangers and aliens, household of God, cornerstone, holy temple, and dwelling place. This overlap isn't incidental. It's integral to understanding how the local church is yet another act in the same story that has been unfolding since Genesis 1.

Where do the travelers and nomads look if they want to know what God is like? They should look to the church. Sure, they can study how individual Christians live. They can see how you treat your family and your coworkers and elected officials, and "they may see your good deeds and glorify God on the day of visitation" (1 Peter 2:12). The church can be—in fact, we must be—the "light of the world" (Matthew 5:14). One Christian is a flashlight. A church is a lighthouse.

There's a reason why Paul tells the Ephesians that "through the church the manifold wisdom of

God might now be made known to the rulers and authorities in the heavenly places" (Ephesians 3:10). There's a reason why Paul encouraged the Corinthian Christians to practice orderly, God-centered worship so that "[if] an unbeliever or outsider enters, he is convicted by all, he is called to account by all, the secrets of his heart are disclosed, and so, falling on his face, he will worship God and declare that God is really among you" (1 Corinthians 14:24–25). The reason is that the church is God's temple, full of God's people, who are working together to live lives of worship that please him.

MANY PEOPLE, ONE BODY

When you became a Christian, you started following Jesus. I hope you also joined a church. Jesus didn't come to earth to live a perfect life, die a sin-atoning death, and rise again so his people would become a horde of disconnected, disparate individuals. He died for his church. He purchased his people. He laid down his life for his sheep. So join a church; publicly identify with the people of God through baptism (Acts 2:38); submit your life to the faithful scrutiny of fellow saints in a single flock under the leadership of faithful undershepherds who love you, who are accountable for you, whose lives you can imitate, and whose counsel you can follow (1 Corinthians 5:12; 1 Peter 5:1–5; Hebrews 13:7, 17).

One day that church, those people, or that flock, will all be gathered as one. Jesus's perfect work will have come to complete fruition. But we're not there yet. Until that day, we wait—not by ourselves, but in faith-filled fellowship with our brothers and sisters in Christ. We gather every Lord's Day to encourage each other to press on in the faith. Here's how the author of Hebrews puts it:

> And let us consider how to stir up one another to love and good works, not neglecting to meet together, as is the habit of some, but encouraging one another, and all the more as you see the Day drawing near. (Hebrews 10:24–25)

Don't neglect the privilege of gathering with the saints. Our churches are gatherings of believers who are committed to help each other follow Jesus and reflect our Savior. We are a royal priesthood, a holy nation. If you neglect the habit of meeting together—and I'm sure you know some Christians who do—you'll be missing out on so much.

The Spirit's Presence and the Church's Place

Earlier in this chapter, we examined Paul's words in 1 Corinthians 3:16—"Do you not know that you are God's temple and that God's Spirit dwells in you?"—and briefly explored that our status as God's temple refers primarily to the gathering of believers, the church. But what about the Spirit's indwelling that Paul also refers to in this verse?

The Holy Spirit absolutely indwells individual believers. In John 14:17, Jesus promises that this will happen. It's mentioned in various ways in various places throughout the New Testament (Romans 8:15–17; Galatians 5:22–23; Ephesians 1:13–14; Titus 3:5). But that's not the focus of this chapter. In fact, I'm willing to say that God dwells among his gathered people in a unique way, in a way that he doesn't dwell among a single Spirit-filled individual.

And so, it's worth asking again: Where do the travelers and nomads look *today* if they want to know what God is like? Where do God's people *today* dwell in peace with him? For those who have faith in Christ, for those who have been saved by Jesus and sealed by the Spirit, the answer should be clear: the local church.

The church is important, but it's not ultimate. Just like the temple and the tabernacle before it, it's meant to be a sign of what Jesus's reign on earth might look like. It's meant to be an on-ramp to otherworldly fellowship. It's meant to be a temporary home for those who are nomads on this earth.

Remember, we gather to encourage one another because "the Day" is drawing near. What day? The day Jesus comes back, and our journey on earth finally ends.

QUESTIONS FOR REFLECTION

1. If you are a believer in Jesus, you are God's temple and belong to the greater temple of God's worldwide church. How does that connection show up in your everyday life?

2. Another metaphor the Bible uses for "church" is a body. Read 1 Corinthians 12 for an example. That passage is *not* about the worldwide church, but a local church in Corinth. Are you meaningfully connected to a local church where you live? Are you known? Do you know your fellow members?

Chapter 10

Revelation 1–22:
The Future

I promised that this would be a book about how God's people get to God's place. We've covered many millennia, this story has had many ebbs and flows, and its travelers have made it through many dangers, toils, and snares, and now we're reaching the end.

This grand journey ends with Jesus coming back to finish what he started in creation itself (John 1:3; Colossians 1:16; Hebrews 1:2). It ends with Jesus coming back to bring his people home. It ends with the foggy and staticky vision of Ezekiel 48 giving way to crystal clarity. It ends with God bringing heaven to earth—and this time, it will stick.

The Lord gives the apostle John a vision of what this will be like:

> Then I saw a new heaven and a new earth, for the first heaven and the first earth had passed away, and the sea was no more. And I saw the holy city, new Jerusalem, coming down out of heaven from God, prepared as a bride adorned for her husband. And I heard a loud voice from the throne saying, "Behold, the dwelling place of God is with man. He will dwell with them, and they will be his people, and God himself will be with them as their God. He will wipe away every tear from their eyes, and death shall be no more, neither shall there be mourning, nor crying, nor pain anymore, for the former things have passed away." (Revelation 21:2–4)

Behold, the dwelling place of God is with man. What does it look like? It looks a lot like the city Ezekiel describes (Revelation 21:9–15). It also looks a lot like a perfected Eden:

> Then the angel showed me the river of the water of life, bright as crystal, flowing from the throne of God and of the Lamb through the middle of the street of the city; also, on either side of the river, the tree of life with its twelve kinds of fruit, yielding its fruit each month. The leaves of the tree were for

the healing of the nations. No longer will there be anything accursed, but the throne of God and of the Lamb will be in it, and his servants will worship him. They will see his face, and his name will be on their foreheads. And night will be no more. They will need no light of lamp or sun, for the Lord God will be their light, and they will reign forever and ever. (Revelation 22:1–5)

The tree of life is there, and in this future its leaves are for the healing of the nations. But nothing needs healing anymore. The curse has been lifted.

It's worth looking at one last snapshot the Lord gives John: "And I saw no temple in the city, for its temple is the Lord God the Almighty and the Lamb. And the city has no need of sun or moon to shine on it, for the glory of God gives it light, and its lamp is the Lamb" (21:22–23).

Did you catch what's *not* there? A temple. Of course there isn't. There's no need for a temple in glory—because the sign has receded and graciously given way to the signifier. There's no need for a temple in glory because the Lord is there, and the Lamb is there.

What gloriously good news. We won't be nomads much longer. Our long, often difficult wandering through the waystation of this life is nearly at an end. Jesus is coming soon. He's coming home to his people.

How does your heart respond to that news? I suppose your response depends entirely on your relationship to the one coming home. If you've received God's grace and mercy and trusted Christ, if you've been reborn by his Spirit and adopted into God's family, then the prospect of his return thrills you.

If that's you, then I encourage you to keep following him on the long road home to glory. Fight temptation because he is worth it. Stake your confidence on his promises because he is worth it. Lock arms with a healthy church who helps you in all this because he is worth it. Sacrifice your time; spend your talents and your resources. Pursue the Lord and his people in all that you do—not so that you will be made righteous on the last day, but because you know you already are declared righteous for the last day because of your faith in God's Son. And when the path home becomes difficult—and it will—pray for his grace, strength, and faithfulness to be with you. He will answer in marvelous ways you cannot comprehend.

But if God is a stranger to you, if his promises leave you cold and unmoved, if you wall yourself off from his people, then I suspect that the prospect of his return holds little sway in your heart. Friend, if that's you, I urge you to consider the uniform testimony of Scripture: Jesus is the Son of God, and his life, death, and resurrection are proof-positive that the Lord always keeps his promises. Whether your journey in this life is short and full of problems, or long and full of relative ease, one day you will die. That day is appointed (Hebrews 9:27), and what's after death is appointed too: judgment.

"He who testifies to these things says, 'Surely I am coming soon.' Amen. Come, Lord Jesus! The grace of the Lord Jesus be with all. Amen" (Revelation 22:20–21).

Now take a deep breath and ask yourself this question: Are you ready?

Questions for Reflection

1. Are you ready for Jesus's return?
2. How does your heart respond to the truth that all followers of Jesus will experience God's intimate presence for all eternity?
3. How does knowing the end of God's great story affect the way you live today?

Acknowledgments

Agreeing to write a book is easy, almost too easy. Writing a book is hard, sometimes too hard, which is why I'm thankful that almost every good book is the fruit of partnership. This writer would be lost without such help.

The person who first comes to mind is Sam Bierig. I'm thankful that he thought of me to contribute to this series. Your witty wisdom gave me confidence. I hope it matches what you're looking for. I'm thankful also for Spurgeon College and Midwestern Seminary's obvious investment in these kinds of projects that don't just appeal to the seminarian.

I'm thankful for the good folks at New Growth Press: Brad Byrd, Ruth Castle, and Barbara Juliani. Your counsel in both concept and content improved this book. Thanks also for the great cover, whoever designed that. I'm particularly grateful for Josh

Cooley, whose perceptive editing made this book both clearer *and* shorter.

I'm thankful for Jim Hamilton and Sam Emadi, who have forever changed the way I read the Bible. I'm thankful for Bob Russell, the long-term pastor of Southeast Christian Church, who is the first preacher I remember. He opened and explained the Bible so that, even as a middle-schooler, I thought to myself, "There's nothing like this book." The Lord saved me under his ministry, and I have no idea where I'd be otherwise.

Finally, the goal of this short book is to take one theme and trace it from beginning to end. There are many books with a similar, even identical aim. There are probably at least one or two that are better than this one. That's okay. The Bible deserves to be endlessly written about and endlessly reflected upon. It's an amazing and profound book. There's nothing like it. It both demands and deserves our attention, and it will repay 1,000-fold whatever attention we give it. So, more than anything else, I hope this book deepened your desire to give attention to the Bible.

Alex Duke
April 2025

Endnotes

INTRODUCTION

1. For the best intro into the topic of the inspiration of Scripture, consider Kevin DeYoung's *Taking God at His Word* (Crossway, 2014).

CHAPTER 1

1. For more on this, see my book *From Eden to Egypt: A Guided Tour of Genesis* (Zondervan Reflective, 2025).

CHAPTER 2

1. Notice that in Genesis 3:21, God covers their shame with clothing. He didn't have to do that. What mercy. He blesses the blasphemers.

CHAPTER 3

1. He gave it to Abraham in Genesis 15:13.

CHAPTER 4

1. By which I mean Genesis, Exodus, Leviticus, Numbers, and Deuteronomy.

2. As I already mentioned, yes, the Lord was "with" all his people who followed him by faith, e.g., Joseph. But his presence was not permanently localized anywhere from Eden until Sinai and then the tabernacle.

CHAPTER 5

1. See *Star Wars: Episode VI—Return of the Jedi*, directed by Richard Marquand (20th Century-Fox, 1983), film.

CHAPTER 7

1. Somewhat confusingly, this king of Israel who captures Amaziah is *also* named Jehoash (2 Kings 14:11–14).

2. That's my colloquialized translation of 2 Kings 20:19.

3. The same thing happened in Israel a century and a half earlier. The author retells it with much less fanfare, since the Northern Kingdom wasn't his primary focus. See 2 Kings 17.

4. Yes, we're skipping the second-temple phase that Ezra and Nehemiah describe. For our purposes, here's what we need to know. Some Jews are granted the opportunity to return from exile and rebuild their temple. When they finally get it

finished, it so pales in comparison that they old men who remember the original one cannot help but to weep (Ezra 3:12–13).

CHAPTER 8

1. Historians generally agree that the first temple was built around 1000 BC. Rome, meanwhile, was founded around 753 BC.